EXTRAVAGANT LOVE

EXTRAVAGANT LOVE

The Self-Emptying of Jesus

RUTH BURROWS
Edited and compiled by Michelle Jones

Paulist Press
New York / Mahwah, NJ

Frontispiece: *The Merciful Trinity* by Sr. M. Caritas Muller, OP. Used with permission. Line drawing by Sr. Elizabeth Obbard of the Quidenham Carmel. Used with permission.

Cover image by agsandrew/Shutterstock.com
Cover design by Sharyn Banks
Book design by Lynn Else

Library of Congress Cataloging-in-Publication Data
Names: Burrows, Ruth, author. | Jones, Michelle, 1976– author.
Title: Extravagant love : the self-emptying of Jesus / Ruth Burrows ; edited and compiled by Michelle Jones.
Description: New York / Mahwah, NJ : Paulist Press, [2022] | Summary: "In baptism we are all plunged into the self-emptying life of Jesus, and we are called to live our lives in this way of love. Ruth Burrows draws together insights from Scripture and theology, as well as her experience as a Carmelite for seventy years"—Provided by publisher.
Identifiers: LCCN 2021032141 (print) | LCCN 2021032142 (ebook) | ISBN 9780809155804 (paperback) | ISBN 9781587689796 (ebook)
Subjects: LCSH: Incarnation—Meditations.
Classification: LCC BT220 .B875 2022 (print) | LCC BT220 (ebook) | DDC 232/.1—dc23
LC record available at https://lccn.loc.gov/2021032141
LC ebook record available at https://lccn.loc.gov/2021032142

ISBN 978-0-8091-5580-4 (paperback)
ISBN 978-1-58768-979-6 (e-book)

Published by Paulist Press
997 Macarthur Boulevard
Mahwah, New Jersey 07430
www.paulistpress.com

Printed and bound in the
United States of America

These meditations on the kenosis of
the Son of God are offered in esteem and
love to Sr. Lydia and to her daughters,
the Sisters of Jesus of Nazareth.

Sr. Rachel, OCD (Ruth Burrows)

CONTENTS

CONTENTS

FOREWORD

The origin story of *Extravagant Love* reflects the theme the book explores. *Extravagant Love* began its life as a wondrous gift of love from Sr. Rachel Gregory (whose pen name is Ruth Burrows) of the Quidenham Carmelite Monastery, UK, to Sr. Lydia Fabian and her community, the Sisters of Jesus of Nazareth, in Chegutu, Zimbabwe. This generous offering was the culmination of over fifteen years of guidance in the spiritual and monastic life that Rachel had poured out upon her "dear African sisters." What a blessed companionship! In Rachel, the Sisters of Jesus of Nazareth—an emerging contemplative community—were gifted with a woman who not only is one of the most compelling and challenging spiritual writers of our time but also was profoundly influential in her monastery in reshaping the enclosed Carmelite life in accordance with the directives of the Second Vatican Council. When Lydia asked Rachel for some reflections on the spirituality of her new community, she never could have foreseen the treasury of wisdom that was lavished upon her and her sisters in response.

The theme of the book is the self-outpouring in love, or the kenosis, of Jesus Christ. The kenosis of the Son of God is at the heart of the identity of the Sisters of Jesus of Nazareth. Their self-understanding and daily lives are centered on sharing intimately in this mystery of extravagant love. In this way, the Chegutu sisters present to the people of God an intense expression of the universal Christian calling. In baptism, we are all plunged into the self-emptying life of Jesus and are called to live out this way of love in whatever situations we find ourselves. It is not surprising, then, that while the book was originally written to benefit a particular religious community, it is, in fact, deeply significant to all followers of Jesus.

Extravagant Love is not a sustained treatise on the kenosis of the Son of God. The mystery is too great for that. Rather, Sr. Rachel draws together scriptural and theological insights and her own lived experience of over seventy years as a Carmelite nun to offer various streams into the unfathomable ocean of God's self-giving, ecstatic love. Each reflection is intended to begin in reading and to continue in prayerful pondering and contemplative wonder.

The Sisters of Jesus of Nazareth continue the outpouring of generous love by allowing a precious personal gift to be made available to a far wider readership. The sisters have never gotten used to the book; it continues to surprise, enrich, and form them and the friends of their community. As we gratefully receive this treasure from their hands, may we open ourselves with trust to being claimed and shaped by the torrent of intimate, unbounded love flowing from the heart of the Son of God.

Michelle Jones

FROM SR. RACHEL TO THE SISTERS OF JESUS OF NAZARETH

Inevitably these reflections are pitifully unworthy of the subject. They do, however, cover a range of biblical and theological material. Each essay introduces several aspects of divine revelation that call for development. The scriptural references and quotations themselves invite loving, eager investigation. I suggest that what I am offering you is a study booklet to provoke and stimulate prayerful pondering, either individually or in community discussion. At least that is my hope. I have done little more than indicate half-opened doors. Go through one and you will find yourself wandering amazed into the mystery of Jesus. Open another and a wholly new vision is spread before you of him who emptied himself in extravagant love for us.

I cannot think of a more wonderful vocation than yours, Sisters of Jesus of Nazareth, whose privilege it is to enter profoundly into the kenosis of the Son of God. Every Christian has this vocation but not all are called to consecrate their entire life to the living of this mystery and fashioning a way of life in which it is expressed day in, day out. As I read your Statutes, I find myself saying, "How beautiful! How beautiful!" At its humble birth and infancy your Association was given the name of The Manger. Whenever I wrote to Sr. Lydia and addressed the envelope to The Manger, I experienced a thrill of pleasure. The choice of name reflected clearly the charism bestowed on Sr. Lydia and her first companions for the "upbuilding" of the Church.

The pattern of your monastic life with its rhythm of Divine Office, *lectio divina*, solitary prayer, labor, and hospitality, in a dignified setting of poverty, when it is characterized by personal humility, simplicity, and absence of all ostentation, opens a door by which you can enter and live within the mystery of Jesus's kenosis. The Charter of your Association stands written on the first page of the Statutes: "Let the same mind be in you that was in Christ Jesus" (Phil 2:5). That mind, that passionate, reckless love for us that caused him to cast aside his divine status as Son with its happiness and glory to assume our fallen condition, the "nature of a slave." He becomes so lowly, so lowly. How can a poor, selfish earthling I know myself to be have such a mind? "You can't," Jesus agrees, "but I can give you my mind, I can live my boundless love in you if you let me." We let him when we do all we possibly can do, living our life faithfully day by day, trying always to please Our Lord and serve our sisters.

Although he is working in us, loving us, giving himself to us whenever we are doing his will, he can do this most powerfully when for a given space of time we lay aside our own "doing" and remain exposed to him in prayer.

Mariachiedza—Mary the Bearer of Light—is your mother. She lays her defenseless Son in the manger of your hearts, pleading with you to cherish him and never, never to wound him. Her gentle, feminine, unobtrusive presence pervades your monastery, secretly lingering and encouraging you in your wonderful, demanding vocation to ensure that the Light, the fire of God's love, is kept burning in your hearts, its radiance hidden from human eyes, covering the vast continent of Africa, and most dearly and nearly, your beloved homeland, Zimbabwe. Each one of you must hold herself responsible for maintaining the purity and beauty of your holy Association, and for passing it on to the next generation. May you spend your lives, my dear African sisters, exploring and living within this mystery that is our earth's heaven.

Sr. Rachel Gregory, OCD (Ruth Burrows)

The Merciful Trinity. Ceramic by Sr. Caritas Müller, OP.

I

WHO IS AS GOD?

Can we believe that God comes so close, is so bound up with us, as this image reveals? See how, of the four connecting circles, the center one is the focus of the other three. Within that circle lies each one of us, helpless. The divine Trinity comes down to our aid, the Father gently lifting us up and tenderly pressing his holy face against our leprous cheek; the Son kneels to kiss our dirty, crippled feet, delighting in being our servant; as a dove in flames, the Spirit, mutual love of Father and Son, swoops down to complete our enfolding into the unspeakable glory of the triune life.

This image powerfully summarizes the mystery of the incarnation. Who could have dreamed that the Creator of the universe, too great for any created mind to comprehend (Isa 40:12–26 and others), would choose to become defenseless as a slave, totally immersed in our feverish, sinful, suffering existence, yearning humbly for our love, prepared to expend himself to win it? So loved are we! So loved! Shall we be his joy and delight, or shall we break his heart?

When we pore over the Gospels, our heart in our eyes, longing to know our beloved Lord; as we watch him, listen to him, we see more and more the true nature of our God, what our God is *really* like. God has revealed himself as pure compassion and love.

Christ Crucified

2

THE SON OF GOD IS IN CHEGUTU

In this reflection on the breathtaking immanence of the incarnate Son of God, we are reminded that Jesus is in Chegutu, the home of the Sisters of Jesus of Nazareth, and wherever any of us are, intimately present to us and yearning for our presence with him.

Imagine someone gave you the startling news,
"The Messiah, the Son of God is in Galilee. He is at the lakeside!"
"The Son of God? Can it be?"
"Come and see."

So we go along. What do we see? A human being! A man! A perfectly ordinary man, his face lined with care, sweat upon his brow; no shining aura around his head. His accent is thoroughly Galilean. Yet see how the sick throng around him, crushing him, reaching out to touch him! His whole being exudes compassion as he moves among them. Eyes grow bright, people laugh aloud, the crippled dance with restored life. Wherever he passes, flowers of joy and hope spring up. God's beautiful but defiled creation is being restored.

How moving to see him travel from place to place, interested in all around him, resting by the wayside, eating, sleeping, smiling, weeping, and at times inexpressibly weary: unmistakably human! Here is the Wisdom of God incarnate, delighting to be with the human family, sharing their life in all its aspects! To compile a list of the common things of human life that Jesus refers to proves a formidable enterprise: fishermen, housewives, a woman in labor, vineyards, hens, eggs, snakes, stones, birds, buds, fruits, digestion, elimination, water, bread—the list goes on. Here on earth is the divine Word, holy Wisdom, by whom and for whom all things were made, experiencing human life at a particular moment in human history, a Jew in Palestine.

He sees with a human heart and a human mind, a heart and mind so steadfastly united to God, so pure, that he sees and understands everything in relation to his beloved Father. No one has ever seen and appreciated as he the wonder and beauty of our world and all that is within it. Dear Lord, share your vision with us!

No longer bound in human limitation, Jesus Christ is yet the same today as yesterday. The Son of God is in Chegutu and in Chinhoyi and wherever you are placed, delighting to be with you, sharing your life to the full. He is there with you in the kitchen, in the cowshed, in the chapel— everywhere. "Do not press me to leave you or to turn back from following you! Where you go, I will go; where you lodge, I will lodge" (Ruth 1:16). This is his plea to *you*. He is with you; are you always with him? To be with Jesus is our life. We cannot truly *be*, we cannot have fullness of being, except we abide in him, draw life from him. Prayer, therefore, is not one activity among others, prayer is our whole life. We must labor to live according to this truth, faithfully giving proper time to prayer, frequently throughout the day adverting to his presence and offering him tokens of love, listening to his mysterious promptings so as to be intent on doing what he wants, seeking his interests not our own.

To foster this personal intimacy and to ensure that the Jesus of our hearts is the real, living Jesus, we need daily recourse to the Gospels. Nothing is more important for each one of us than to *labor* to know Jesus, to respond to the intimacy he offers to each one of us. We must be *rooted* in him, *grounded* in love so as to draw life from the very Fount of love (see Eph 3:17). Only if we live in Jesus and he lives his life in us, can we give him to others.

3

REJOICE IN
THE LORD

Ecce homo! Behold the true human being, the only one! What is a human being? "It is that," says Karl Rahner, "which appears when God wishes to express himself outside himself." Jesus is the perfect self-expression of God: Light from Light, true God from true God. The story of Jesus, his life, suffering, and death, is nothing other than the projection into our sinful world of the triune life of God. Let us listen to the weighty words with which the evangelist John opens his account of the passion: "Jesus knew that his hour had come to depart from this world and go to the Father. Having loved his own who were in the world, he loved them to the end," that is, to the uttermost extent of love. "Knowing that the Father had given all things into his hands, and that he had come from God and was going to God, he got up from the table, took off his outer robe, and tied a towel around himself. Then he poured water into a basin and began to wash the disciples' feet" (John 13:1, 3–5). Though he was in the form of God, he did not count equality with God a thing to be grasped and held on to. Rather he willingly emptied himself of it, taking the form of a servant and humbling himself even unto death (see Phil 2:6–8).

God is not the eternal celibate. God is ecstatic, passionate, out-flowing love that cannot be contained, whose very nature is communion, self-communication. When pure, unprotected, uncontainable love is loose in the world such as we have made it, we have the Son of Man mocked, scourged, spat upon, and crucified. But love does not turn in on itself, does not cease to be love and proves mightier than pain and death; it swallows them up and emerges triumphant. *Ecce homo!*

In Jesus we see the life of God lived humanly. God's life is not God's alone; it is ours also. This is our inheritance, for this we were made, chosen before the foundation of the world to be in communion with God and with all others. "That they may all be one. As you, Father, are in me and I am in you, may they also be in us" (John 17:21). In spite of all appearances, in the very midst of our abounding weakness, we are *enabled* to live God-life, to be for others, ecstatic, willingly laying down our life. Impossible of ourselves! The very love that drives out fear, love that affords absolute security, is what we dread. We want to protect ourselves from it, wrap ourselves up in ourselves and, as I saw on a church notice board, "Someone wrapped up in self makes a very small parcel." But the Spirit of God has been poured into our hearts. Through the out-pouring of Jesus in death, we are delivered from all bonds. It is up to us to walk free.

We are true human persons only when we are outside ourselves, living for others, because this is to be living God-life, caught up into the holy communion with God. But as we see clearly, there is no living in love without pain, the pain of being human. For one thing, we do not see others as they really are. If we did, if we could see as God sees, there would be no problem, we would be on our knees, enraptured, but—*ecce homo*! Yet what is there to see in Jesus himself but a sight from which we long to turn away our eyes, nothing there to attract our gaze? Only the eyes of faith and love see the radiant light, the Son divine of God the Father's deathless face. So it is with one another, so it is with our own selves.

There is, I think, a particular aspect of pain that gets neglected in that it is deemed too mean, shameful even, to form part of what we are happy to offer to God. It is an incommunicable pain having to do just with me being me and a me I do not like. Instinctively we contrast this unclaimed pain with "real" suffering: bereavement, oppression, torture, hunger, imprisonment, illness, and so on, and we feel still more ashamed and self-despising. Some of us know this about ourselves but some, I think, do not and therefore this particular pain, so precious, I believe, in God's eyes, is not exposed to him and so it blocks our capacity for wholehearted love; we are that much less a person. The pain may be precisely the inability to accept self. Let us take every aspect of our human experience and spread it out to God without fear, without shame.

"*Ecce homo!*" we may say, and without any doubt we shall hear the answer: "My beloved!" Jesus, looking into his heart, saw nothing but his Father's love, and from and in that love he lived and died. So each of us, if we would turn eyes of faith into ourselves, would see only God's love and choose that as our ground, our source, and empowering.

4

LOWLY WILL
HIS CRADLE BE

"God from God, Light from Light, true God from true God," whom dominions worship, before whom the powers of heaven tremble and the seraphim veil their faces, in becoming human espouses from beginning to end what is poor, humble, lowly. Scripture and the liturgy speak of "descending," "coming down." These expressions are, of course, metaphorical, another way of saying, "being rich he became poor"—for our sake. He leaves his Father's heaven, lays aside his glory, and comes into this world with no defenses from the hazards, the hardships, and agonies of human life. His life begins as every human life begins, an embryo developing in Mary's womb.

We find ourselves dumbfounded, do we not? Who could have believed such a thing! The Son of God, by whom all things were made, for whom all things were made, has himself become made, "ungodded," in the womb of a village girl of no consequence. With the eternal God on earth, now of the earth, inseparably united with it, the transformation of creation has begun. Earth did not rock on its foundation or the mountains skip like lambs, the world rolled on its course and men and women went about their daily rounds as before, wholly oblivious that human life, human history had changed forever.

Not "clothed with honor and majesty, wrapped in light as with a garment" (Ps 104:1-2) did he come into his world, the king of kings! No golden cradle, softly lined, awaited him. The princely Babe was born in a stable and laid in the animals' feeding trough. We see a stark foreshadowing of the hard road he would tread to his death on the wood of a cross to become the Bread of Life for humankind, that living Bread without which we cannot live. The "lowly of the earth," shepherds and simple village folk, surround his cradle, the "mighty of the earth" being otherwise engaged.

That the great angel-blinding Light should
   shrink

His blaze to shine in a poor shepherd's eye,
That the unmeasured God so low should sink
As pris'ner in a few poor rags to lie....
That glory's Self should serve our griefs and
     fears,
And free Eternity submit to years....
     (Richard Crashaw)

Throughout the Gospel narratives, we see the incarnate Lord's predilection for what is lowly, in the world's estimation unimportant, even worthless. The reputation of being a miracle-worker distressed him, and he begged those whom he cured not to publicize the fact. Jesus was totally concerned with his Father's interests, not at all with himself. He shunned praise: "Why do you ask me about what is good? There is only one who is good" (Matt 19:17). Unassuming, endlessly serving, abhorring ostentation, poor, gentle, self-expending, such was the human life of God.

The Incarnate Word's way of living confronts us with an awesome insight into the very nature of God. "God is love" (1 John 4:16) and God loves with a love of which our human love, even at its purest and deepest, is but a faint echo. True love is always humble, vulnerable, tremulously offering itself, incapable of force, and freely exposed to hurt and rejection; rejected, "love lies bleeding." Love is self-gift and therefore self-emptying. Jesus's kenosis, his "ecstasy" of love for his Father, and his Father's love for Jesus, "my Son and the delight of my heart," reveal that the Holy Trinity is a mystery of self-giving, ecstatic love, a selflessness that is the cause of all that is. We are made in the image of God and selfless love must be the heartbeat of our life also.

5

THE WONDER OF MY BEING

It was you who formed my inward parts;
  you knit me together in my mother's
  womb.
I praise you, for I am fearfully and
  wonderfully made. (Ps 139:13-14)

It is by God's perfect will that each one of us exists: "I want *you*. Be!" Existence is pure gift. "I" was not there to ask to be given existence and life! Have you from time to time, or even once, been confronted with the astounding *fact*: "I *am*, but I *need not be*! I am *receiving* existence from my Creator! How close he is to me!" Normally we take ourselves for granted, but moments of awed realization are precious.

Our life on earth begins as a tiny, helpless scrap of humanity, totally dependent on others for the maintenance of life. From the very first we are conditioned. We do not choose our parentage and all that involves in the way of race, homeland, and culture. Our genes may be strong and healthy or they may be defective. Our temperament is not of our choosing. Like all mammals on earth, given right conditions, our physical being develops without any conscious intervention on our part. There comes a moment however, when we human beings can *choose* and it is then that the great drama of our personal life begins, a drama of such magnitude that only God can fully comprehend.

Created by Love and for Love, nothing on earth can ever fully satisfy us. Still, we are creatures of earth, we love it, it is our home, the maternal womb in which we are nourished and by which our needs are answered. Yet our deepest heart has a need that earth cannot fulfill, the need for God. We are of this world, adapted to it, drawn to it, yet called to a destiny that is beyond all created capacity to attain. This is our basic poverty. We *are* a yearning, an emptiness crying out to be filled by God. We long for something we have not got and, what is more, cannot get.

No such longings trouble the other inhabitants of our world. Their instincts direct them of necessity to their fulfillment within this world:

born, they grow to maturity, reproduce, and die. Our grandeur and our pain is that, as creatures of the earth, our destiny is transcendent, beyond what we can know or, of ourselves, attain. Only God can bring us to God. We must allow him to, and Jesus shows us the way, the way of obedience.

Jesus's fundamental obedience that comprised all his distinct acts was to *accept* his humanity and experience without evasion the poverty and pain of being human. Each one of us is faced with the same choice: our Creator's loving will for us or the vain pursuit of a fulfillment within this world. Though in prayerful moments we sincerely determine to choose God's holy will, as our life unfolds day by day, we encounter the attraction of earthly things, the things seen rather than the things unseen and known only by faith.

Constantly to choose in all the details of our life what faith shows us to be the will of God is impossible for us as of ourselves. The kenosis of Jesus alone enables us to do the impossible, to win the victory over our intense egotism, the self-centeredness that wants what *I* want here and now, the pride that claims independence. "Apart from me you can do nothing" (John 15:5).

Original sin is precisely a rejection of the true reality of our humanity, which is to be a *capax Dei* (capacity for God). As yet we are only in the process of becoming human. We will be truly human when we are filled with the fullness of God. That can only be by denying our egotism and "letting" God, that is, by surrendering to his will. Jesus's life was one of total obedience to the Father's will even to a terrible, shameful death, to the loss of all that seemed to make him human—he was emptied. That is why the Father raised him to the heights, filling his emptiness with himself (see Phil 2:9). Obedience is faith and love in act.

In Jesus we see our path. He did not write his own script for the drama of his life and neither do we write ours. The part we must play is given to us. Our life's task is to devote ourselves to this, to be what God wants us to be, that unique, irreplaceable delight of his heart.

Christ Crucified

6

WISDOM NOT
OF THIS AGE

In my very young days, I, like many people at the time, held a view of Jesus that did not, could not, take with total seriousness the reality of his humanity. Somehow his "Godness" was always there, "interfering" in a reassuring way when needed, reassuring to Jesus himself and of course reassuring to us. Well-instructed, we knew of the Docetic heresy but failed to perceive that it informed our devotional life. In the decades of the second half of the last century and at the present time, Christian theology has counteracted this danger with its unequivocal assertion of the reality of Jesus's humanity. His consciousness, his mind, his will were purely human. Divine attributes never intruded into this pure humanity. Jesus's mind, no matter how elevated, was finite.

It seems to me that too easily we avoid the impact of the awesome word *became*. God *became* something that he was not before. Expressed in our pitifully inadequate words, God *began* to have an experience other than that of being God. He did not merely *clothe* himself in human flesh; there was no shadow of pretense—God *became* flesh. The Son of God, Word of the Father, *learned* in bitter suffering how hard it was to be the Son of Man and to die. No wonder we waver and shrink from the implications of this. Yet herein lies our path to glory. We ourselves learn what it is to be truly human, to love our humanity, loyally embrace it as he did. More importantly, we gain from Jesus the love, the willing obedience, by which to remain true to our humanity.

To us has been imparted the secret wisdom that is not of this age or of the rulers of this age, a wisdom that is for our glorification: Christ crucified, the wisdom and the power of God (see 1 Cor 1-2). The "natural" person, and even the natural spiritual person, inevitably conceives an ideal of human perfection. In the Jewish tradition taken over by the Christian Church, Adam and Eve were created in flawless beauty, in radiant perfection, and endowed with preternatural gifts. Only too often, much spiritual striving was, and still is, expended in trying to achieve something of this supposed perfection, to be "as gods."

When God's Messiah, his beloved, his delight, comes among us, surely we will see in him the epitome of human grandeur and bask in reflected glory! Such is the inherited, ineradicable human longing. Yes, truly we will see the perfection of human being, a perfection that is in shocking contrast to the creation of our human pride. The "wisdom of this age" rejected this most holy humanity and continues to do so. None of us can ever presume that we are totally immune to the ancestral sinful pride that desires to be like God, that is, to our own idea of God.

The lowly Son of God, Jesus of Nazareth, shows us what it is to be like God and to live like God in this world. God has made it clear that nothing less is worthy of the creatures he has made in his own image. Let us never take our eyes off his Son. No other model suffices.

Christ Crucified

7

YOUR WILL IS MY DELIGHT

"My food is to do the will of him who sent me." (John 4:34)

The evangelist John makes blazingly explicit the heartbeat of Jesus's existence: the Father's will. "I can do nothing on my own. As I hear, I judge; and my judgment is just, because I seek to do not my own will but the will of him who sent me" (John 5:30); "I have come down from heaven, not to do my own will, but the will of him who sent me" (John 6:38). Quotations could be multiplied; the entire Gospel must be read to illustrate the totality of Jesus's surrender to the Father. He is devoid of egotism, emptied of self-will. The eyes of his heart are on the Father, his ears straining to listen. It would be a mistake, I think, to assume that Jesus had unequivocal directions straight from his Father. If that were so, he would not be like us in every way except sin.

Rather, the Father's will was communicated to him in a way similar to how it is communicated to us. It would be manifested in events, through the voice and action of others, and by the mysterious inner intuitions that come to us on rare occasions, directing us firmly on a particular course. There are many instances in our lives when the Father's will is unmistakable, yet this is not always so and we must make a decision without the comforting certainty that it is the right one. Jesus too would know this uncertainty, yet know too how to go forward confidently in the shadows, certain of God's tender love for him, and we learn from him how to do the same. A child makes many mistakes and is no less loved for that.

As a twelve-year-old boy he seems to have assumed that he had a mission to fulfill that involved his remaining in Jerusalem and that his parents were aware of this; after all, the Scriptures offered precedents in the great prophets Samuel and Jeremiah. He was utterly surprised, therefore, by his parents' incomprehension, by their anxiety and reproach. Was he mistaken, then, in assuming that his Father wanted him in Jerusalem? Jesus was a human boy with the ardor and energy of youth, and youth's eagerness to "get-going" in the world. Already he had a profound relationship with his Father and wisdom that amazed his elders. Is it inconceivable that he experienced a longing to preach of what he knew? His parents intervened. "He went down with them and came to Nazareth, and was obedient to them" (Luke 2:51). He went *down* with them.

How pregnant the "down"! The eternal Word descends into the Virgin's womb; the Word Incarnate descends from youthful prominence in the holy city to anonymity in lowly village life. From being an extraordinary youth he became an ordinary one in an obscure village. Instead of publicly voicing his inspired wisdom, he applied himself to learning the carpenter's trade. A window opens for us and through it we glimpse something of the divine splendor and the grandeur of ordinary human life!

We humans are adept at self-deception. The opening prayer of the Mass for the First Week in Ordinary Time is essentially as follows:

In your love, Lord,
give us the grace to know your will
and the strength to do it.

There is scarcely a more important request. "Lord, that I may see." How earnestly we must pray that the eyes of our heart be purified! "Take the veil from my eyes, Lord!"

How pure the hearts of Jesus's parents, transparent to God's holy will! Scripture tells us of Joseph's sensitivity to God's word and his ready will to do it. His mother "pondered all these things in her heart" (Luke 2:19), listened with supreme attention to the Father's word and acted on it. Their young son, Jesus, could readily accept that what his holy parents willed for him surely echoed the will of his heavenly Father.

8

OUR BROTHER

"He committed no sin, and no deceit was found in his mouth" (1 Pet 2:22), yet he let himself be counted as a sinner (see Isa 53:12). We ourselves readily acknowledge, "I have greatly sinned, through my fault, through my fault, through my most grievous fault," but are we ready to accept that other people think us sinners or less than good? We don't like it, do we? We strike our breast and declare ourselves unworthy servants, but resent that others underestimate us and fail to see how good and generous we are. Such is our sensitive human heart, so longing to be esteemed! Let us go to our dearest Lord, watch him, and ask to be taken into his meek and humble heart.

"Then the people of Jerusalem and all Judea were going out to John the Baptist, and all the region along the Jordan, and they were baptized by him in the river Jordan, confessing their sins" (Matt 3:5-6). The sinless Lamb of God joins this throng of sinners on their way to a baptism of repentance. His presence among them made no stir, utterly unaware as they were that divine holiness itself was rubbing shoulders with them, seeing in him only a fellow Israelite roused to repentance by the prophet's preaching. The Holy Spirit revealed his identity to John, and he protested, "I need to be baptized by you, and do you come to me?" (Matt 3:14). Jesus insisted and prevailed for "he had to become like his brothers and sisters in every respect" (Heb 2:17).

Oh, how *real* was the Son of God's *identity* with us in our sin-damaged state! It would have been a relatively small thing to have taken a human nature of untarnished purity and perfect integrity; it was quite another to take it as it actually is, as we know it to be: flawed, "subject to weakness" (Heb 5:2), vulnerable to temptation and moral conflict, subject to bodily pain and ultimately to death. Truly, the Son of God "emptied himself" (Phil 2:7). I do not think Jesus was pretending, acting out the part of a sinner for our edification. His identity with us was such as to make him feel himself in some way soiled by sin.

We recall the long years of obscurity preceding his public ministry. The idea that the Holy Family, consisting merely of Jesus, Mary, and Joseph, lived a quasi-monastic life, separated from the hubbub of village life, is denied by the Gospel narratives that tell us of a large family of boys and girls. There is evidence that they were far from insightful in regard to their brother, Jesus, and possibly somewhat jealous. But what large family of children exists without evidence of human sinfulness—squabbles, rivalries, and selfishness in its various guises?

The Church has always maintained that Our Blessed Lady remained a virgin. We do not know the origin of Jesus's "brothers and sisters." The explanation I favor is grounded on the fact that Our Lady had a sister who was with her on Calvary. What if she were widowed early and she with her children became one family with the Holy Family, to such an extent that the cousins were thought to be brothers and sisters? It is unimportant.

What is important is that by the time of his baptism, Jesus had experience of human sin within a large family, not grave, perhaps, but sin all the same. As a working man, taking orders, exchanging money, he would be fully exposed to humankind in its neighborliness and goodness but also in its selfishness, dishonesty, craftiness, and cruelty. How could the sinless one not feel sin-stained? It

has been given to holy people to experience something of the sin of the world, and they have been
all but crushed by it. What then of Jesus with his
unique knowledge and love of the Father and the
Father's heart?

Take us, spotless Lamb of God, into your meek
and humble heart.

CHRIST CRUCIFIED

9

IMPOVERISHED FOR YOUR SAKE

"And just as he was coming up out of the water, he saw the heavens torn apart and the Spirit descending like a dove on him. And a voice came from heaven, 'You are my Son, the Beloved; with you I am well pleased.' And the Spirit immediately drove him out into the wilderness. He was in the wilderness forty days, tempted by Satan." (Mark 1:10–13)

What a moment for the humble man of Nazareth, seeing heaven opened and hearing the Father's voice acclaiming him as his beloved Son, the delight of his heart! A moment of pure bliss; a moment only, and one swiftly to be left behind as the Spirit drives him into the wilderness to be tempted by Satan. There is clearly a close connection between Jesus's public inauguration as Messiah and his temptations. What is to be the shape of his messianic identity and mission? In reverence and prayer, we try to understand a little of this awesome desert sojourn of God's holy Son.

"It is not good that the man should be alone" (Gen 2:18). On all levels he needs sustenance from other creatures, and this needful sustenance the desert denies him. So deprived, he is faced with the naked poverty of his being, trembling over the abyss of nothingness, feeling himself an emptiness, a boundless need crying out in loneliness. For our sake, Jesus endures this profound human impoverishment in a desolate silence that is broken not by the longed-for Father's voice but by the voice of Satan.

To say that someone is tempted implies that they experience conflict, feel a desire for what their conscience tells them they may not have. Though the temptations assailing Jesus are threefold in form, the underlying factor in all three is Satan's pressure on Jesus to ease his own inner poverty and, with spectacular signs, be the kind of Messiah the people want, putting to use the special powers with which he is endowed for his mission. "Away with you, Satan!" (Matt 4:10), so Jesus utterly rejected the temptation. He understood that his earthly task was to reveal the Father and by this revelation of divine compassion alone to win the hearts of his people to the Father. "I know the Father" (John 10:15), Jesus could confidently assert. He is the Father's Word, the perfect human expression of the Father. All he does, the very way he is, must reflect the selfless love of the Father. In Jesus, we glimpse in the Godhead itself a Self-expenditure, a Self-poured-out, what we might call poverty. For Jesus to betray the poverty of his humanity would be to betray his Father and to betray us.

"He became obedient to the point of death" (Phil 2:8). The essence of Jesus's obedience was acceptance of the humanity he had been given, the consequences that flowed from it, and the mission with which he was entrusted. We see throughout his ministry instances when the temptation was renewed, human voices echoing Satan's. How great must have been the pressure on Jesus's heart that made him cry out, "You faithless generation, how much longer must I be among you? How much longer must I put up with you?" (Mark 9:19). Bear with us he did, staying with us to the bitter end. "For the one who sanctifies and those who are sanctified all have one Father" (Heb 2:11)—in Adam and Eve who despised and denied their humanity and wanted to be "as gods." Yet he who was in the very form of

God disregarded that divine form in order to share fully our flawed humanity, thus in his own person revealing the hidden potentiality of the poverty we so despise.

Naturally speaking, we hate our weaknesses, our limitations, the awareness of our poverty, wanting to feel secure, in control, independent, and self-sufficient. We would like to feel, "I am rich, I have prospered, and I need nothing," while all the time we are faced with the unpleasant reality of being "wretched, pitiable, poor, blind, and naked" (Rev 3:17). Jesus has shown us that this poverty is, in fact, our most precious treasure. "Though he was rich, yet for your sakes he became poor, so that by his poverty you might become rich" (2 Cor 8:9). Oh, how rich, for "blessed are the poor in spirit, *for theirs is the kingdom of heaven*" (Matt 5:3)!

10

OUR HERO

Jesus, the sinless Son sent by the Father "in the likeness of *sinful* flesh" (Rom 8:3), had as his specific earthly mission the restoration of Israel to its vocation to be God's holy people, in whom and through whom God would reign. The nations of the world, perceiving the wisdom, happiness, and godliness of this people, would themselves come to know the God of Israel. Jesus understood that his mission was limited to Israel, only to Israel. No one can claim to know just how Jesus felt and thought, how and when the understanding of his mission changed, but we who love him can keep close to him, ponder his sacred words and actions, and pray to be taken into his mind and heart and to understand what he wants us to understand. We know that he was to be the whole world's Savior, the only Savior, bringing back to the Father his beloved lost, sinful, suffering world. To do this he must allow himself to be plunged into dark, turgid depths, experience in unutterable dismay the horror of human evil. Who can fathom the immeasurable depths of pain into which he sank? "For our sake God *made him to be sin*" (2 Cor 5:21). What depths of abasement for the Holy One of God! "Christ redeemed us from the curse of the law by *becoming a curse* for us" (Gal 3:13).

We sense the joyousness with which Jesus began the task his Father had assigned to him, and we feel with pain the growing animosity of the Pharisees, the superficiality of the crowd's enthusiasm, and the sad incomprehension of those closest to him. Aware of his failure to achieve the hoped-for restoration, Jesus persevered nonetheless, using his fine intelligence, his understanding of the human mind and heart, and his brilliant mastery of the art of preaching, arguing patiently with the intellectualizing Pharisees, talking simply with ordinary folk, pursuing what seemed a thankless, unrewarding task.

Jesus read the signs and knew well that to continue on his present course would bring him to a violent death. He looked to his Father to whom his mission belonged and who directed his course, and knew he must go on, obedient unto death. Yes, death, but only at the appointed time. Jesus surrendered all initiative to his Father; he was "Yes," always "Yes." "Jesus Christ...was not 'Yes and No'; but in him it is always 'Yes'" (2 Cor 1:19). "Jesus began to show his disciples that he must go to Jerusalem and undergo great suffering at the hands of the elders and chief priests and scribes" (Matt 16:21), the personal contribution of these dignitaries being to spit in his face and slap his cheeks as if he were a despicable slave.

These are the religious leaders of God's people, their eminent theologians, guardians of the sacred covenant between God and Israel! Imagine the scene! What hate burned in their hearts that they should so demean themselves! How they feared this mysterious man, powerful even now in his powerlessness, else why abuse him? With this outrageous behavior in the highest religious court, the passion of Jesus began.

"They will hand him over to the Gentiles to be *mocked*" (Matt 20:19). Mockery is a very special and cruel form of torture, attacking a person's sense of self. It is an attempt to undermine, to destroy the personality, to shatter a person's self-respect. The Lord of Glory was subject to every kind of mockery, from the coarse, brutal ribaldry of the soldiers to being ridiculed as a figure of fun by King Herod and his court. Unbearable physical suffering, utter exhaustion, copious bleeding, reduced the "most handsome of men" (Ps 45:2) to a pitiful spectacle, to the satisfaction of his enemies. Tortured, writhing in pain, consumed with anguish...how they relished their victory, enjoyed their last taunt, "'You who would destroy the temple and build it in three days, save yourself! If you are the Son of God, come down from the cross.' In the same way the chief priests also, along with the scribes and elders, were mocking him, saying, 'He saved others; he cannot save himself'" (Matt 27:40–42). To the onlookers, he was indeed as one cursed by God.

All this and more the Church recognizes in the prophetic symbol of Jesus's immersion in the waters of the river Jordan. Bearing our sins in his own body (see 1 Pet 2:24), he sinks down, down, down into his redeeming passion and death. Drowning our sins as Pharaoh's army was drowned, Jesus rises up, not alone but with the "children God has given me" to see heaven torn open and to hear the Father's joyful welcome to his long-lost children. "For the one who sanctifies and those who are sanctified all have one Father. For this reason Jesus is not ashamed to call them brothers and sisters, saying...'Here am I and the children whom God has given me'" (Heb 2:11–13).

II

ONLY BELIEVE

Throughout his ministry Jesus was harassed by taunting, malicious requests for a sign "from heaven": manna falling from the sky, for example— "*then* we will believe that you are from God and speak and act in his name!" (see John 6:30–31). These demands distress Jesus: "he sighed deeply in his spirit" (Mark 8:12); "an evil and adulterous generation asks for a sign" (Matt 16:4). No sign of this kind will be given. Such a prodigy would not create faith in the living, true God, only foster illusions.

Jesus's friends, his brothers also, press him to "manifest" himself to people in general, and especially to the authorities in Jerusalem. They believe not in the real Jesus but in their idea of him.

The lowly Son of Man, endlessly serving, totally expended in concern for his Father's unhappy, misguided, wounded children, *is God's absolute, definitive sign*. Because he is utterly poor, nothing obscures the Father's likeness. Every word, every gesture of Jesus, reveals to us in our mortal state the true and living God, the God of absolute love. No earthly trapping, no material glory or splendor, could contain, let alone express, his transcendent beauty, his radiant glory. To dress him up in our ideas of godlike glory would be akin to Herod's mockery of him, arraying him in gorgeous apparel (see Luke 23:11). It is Jesus in his stark poverty, helpless as the poor are helpless, rejecting everything that could minimize the nakedness of his humanity, who is the human image of God who, though dwelling in inaccessible light, is yet wholly surrendered to his creatures.

If only we could grasp that our own poverty echoes that of Jesus how we would love it, realizing that it is our greatest treasure! We would cease longing for "signs and wonders," what we think are proof of God's interest in us, of his presence and closeness to us. Inevitably we form ideas of holiness, of what it feels like to be close to God, and we are troubled and discontented because we do not feel holy or even good but see ourselves shabby, sinful, and still worldly. Something should be happening, but it isn't happening! What is wrong?

What should I do to get things happening? The answer is simply to set your heart on pleasing God, on doing his will and ignoring yourself as much as you can. Leave your soul in God's hands. We cannot make ourselves holy. Holiness is Jesus living in us, and he cannot live his life in us whilst we cling to our own life.

The only way is to accept our spiritual inadequacies and offer them to Our Lord. O foolish and slow of heart to believe in Jesus, in his words, his promises. Jesus is given to us, he is ours, and we can humbly lay claim to his faith, his love, his total fidelity. Provided you are really trying and can honestly say that there is nothing you know God is asking of you and you are refusing, you can lay aside all anxiety. Be certain that Jesus is with you, the answer to all your desires, to your fears and distress. Our very weaknesses and failings draw him to us, as we see clearly in the Gospels. I believe nothing gives him more joy than bold trust in his merciful love for us no matter what we feel like or how we see ourselves. After all, he knows we are but dust!

"O do let us keep far away from all that glitters!" St. Thérèse of Lisieux writes to her troubled sister. "Let us love our poverty and be content not to have a satisfying spiritual life, not to be pleased with ourselves" (St. Thérèse of Lisieux). When spiritual consolations of one kind or another come your way, receive them gratefully for Our Lord sees you need them to spur you on to greater generosity. What a mistake it is to imagine that consolations are the "real thing" and to be the recipient of such favors means you are advanced or maybe holy, whereas drab prayer is not real prayer at all, merely the way mediocre people have to go. "Poor" prayer from which you get no satisfaction is real prayer, and in it Jesus is offering himself to you.

If the blindness to his reality of his adversaries as well as of his friends so grieves him, revealing as it does an unacknowledged atheism, for "everyone who has heard and learned from the Father comes to me" (John 6:45), our believing without seeing, our trusting him in the dark, gives him immense joy. To remain faithful day in day out to prayer that seems to give you nothing is to embrace Jesus "despised and rejected" (Isa 53:3). It is to be one of those who continue with Jesus in his trials (see Luke 22:28).

12

THE PAIN
AND GLORY OF
BEING HUMAN

Jesus's fundamental earthly task, in which he gave full expression to his love for his Father, was simply to be human, to accept our human lot to the full. Son of God though he was, Jesus learned obedience, learned by sheer experience how hard it is to be human and have to die. Through total acceptance of his human destiny, Jesus was made perfect. The cost was bitter, ending in a cruel, humiliating death, but through it he is able to bring us all along with him to our fulfillment (perfection), provided we accept it as he did. There is only one path to glory and that is the way Christ took—accepting fully the pain of being human (see Heb 5:7–10).

We cannot help but be a member of the human species, but it rests entirely with us whether or not we grow into full humanity, becoming a true man or woman. To be human means we are dependent by our very essence not only for bodily survival, but we also have to look outside ourselves for our meaning. We have no fulfillment within ourselves. Moreover, we know that we are answerable not merely to ourselves but to another outside our control. Our existence is given without our previous consent, our heredity and all that goes with it. We are frighteningly, pitifully, dependent, in countless ways at the mercy of forces beyond our control, vulnerable to what seem tricks of fortune.

Nevertheless, we are answerable. In all our lack of freedom and conditioning, we are responsible for every thought, word, and deed every day of our life and no one can deprive us or relieve us of this responsibility. We ourselves have not written the script for the great drama of our life and the part we must play is assigned to us. Our duty is to play it to the very best of our ability. Jesus's life task and ours are the same: to live out our own individual, unique life with its particular amalgam of characteristics, gifts, defects whether of body or mind, in the circumstances in which we are placed, in love of God and of our neighbor, bearing all things, hoping all things, enduring all things. We have to embrace the painful condition of dependency even when it presses most sorely, never trying to pretend it is other than it is, never railing against it, but accepting it in humble, trustful obedience to the Father and through this loving obedience filtering out all that is evil, transforming it into gold.

At every turn of life, we come up against our limitations. Morally, we fail. We are ignorant and make mistakes, even with the best will in the world, and the consequences of these mistakes can be terrible and far-reaching, affecting not only ourselves but many others. Though Jesus never committed sin, we have no reason for thinking that he never knew the agony of indecision, the agony of doubt: Have I made a mistake? Have I failed in my mission through error of judgment? Have my dealings with the Pharisees been too abrasive? Like us, he had nothing to lean on but the love and fidelity of his Father. Our Father knows of what we are made. He knows our limitations and that sin and mistakes are inevitable. We trust him. He knows what he is doing in his dealings with his beloved human sons and daughters. The destiny toward which he is leading them is beyond the human mind to conceive, surpassing immeasurably our insatiable longing for happiness.

Our pride urges us to escape as much as we can from whatever forces upon us our fundamental state of dependency and helplessness; love for Jesus will make us understand and embrace it, and in it find freedom. How we shrink from little humiliations, from feeling foolish because of some failure! We can give ourselves up to frantic activity to keep at bay an irrational anxiety, a feeling that we are spiritual failures. The answer to all anxiety is acceptance of our basic fragility and poverty and spiritual inadequacies, recognizing a hidden glory in what we fear and despise. Our poverty and dependence are the outward sign, the "sacrament," of our profound, essential relation to God. We are an emptiness only God can fill. Human existence is meaningless apart from this relationship with God.

The pain underlying all our pain is *lack*. We want God! We pine to be united to our Source and to our sole fulfillment. All through his life Jesus accepted this human emptiness, an existence meaningless save in its relation to God. The Father's will was the driving force of his life. He existed by the Father, had nothing of his own, everything was received. "Behold the Man!" Jesus is *the* fulfilled human being and what is true of him must become true of us. To be holy means that a human being has so affirmed, stood by, embraced their essential meaning of being a capacity for God, an emptiness for God to fill, that God has filled them with the fullness of himself.

Christ Crucified

13

A GARDEN FOR GOD

I made a garden for God.
No, do not misunderstand me,
it was not on some lovely estate
or even in a pretty suburb,
I made a garden for God
in the slum of my heart:
a sunless space between grimy walls
the reek of cabbage water in the air
refuse strewn on the cracked asphalt—
the ground of my garden!
This was where I labored
night and day
over the long years
in dismal smog and cold—
there was nothing to show for my toil.

Like a child I could have pretended:
my slum transformed...
an oasis of flowers and graceful trees,
how pleasant to work in such a garden!
I could have lost heart
and neglected my garden
to do something else for God,
but I was making a garden for God
not for myself, for his delight not mine,
and so I worked on in the slum of my heart.
Was he concerned with my garden?
Did he see my labor and tears?
I never saw him looking
never felt him there.
Yet I knew (though it felt as if I did not know)
that he was there with me
waiting...
He has come into his garden,
is it beautiful at last?
Are there flowers and perfumes?
I do not know
the garden is not mine but his—
God asked only for my little space
to be prepared and given;
this is garden for him
and my joy is full.

Christ Crucified

14

JESUS, OUR ALL

Imagine a blissfully happy married couple finding all they need in one another. For no other reason than generosity and the desire to share their happiness, they decide to adopt children as their own. From then on their life undergoes a profound change. Now they are vulnerable. Their happiness depends on the welfare of their children; things can never be the same again. Though still deeply in love, they are "outside themselves," "ecstatic," wrapped up in their children. If the children choose to alienate themselves and start on the path to ruin, the couple are stricken to the heart. They will plead, humble themselves, sacrifice themselves, suffer for and with these cherished sons and daughters, do anything to make them understand that the home is still their home and is waiting for them and that the love they have been given is unchanging.

Does this image give us a little insight into what we call redemption? St. Paul and the liturgy speak of "adoption": we are God's "adopted children"; whereas the evangelist John is emphatic: we *are* God's children now. In some way we share God's genes; divine blood flows within us. The sap of the vine runs through the branches and the vine is one with its branches. There is no vine without its branches and the branches derive from the vine (see John 15:4). Jesus is God's total, unbreakable involvement with us. Never can God be "pure" God again; he remains ever and ever God-with-humanity-in-his-heart. Humanity is within the Godhead for ever and ever.

In Jesus we see that there are no limits to what God is for us. No servanthood equals his. He does not merely supply our needs; he is himself everything we need and entirely at our disposal. He is our life's sun, banishing our darkness and vitalizing our powers of growth. As a loving shepherd, he leads us along the right way, tending our wounds, sheltering, pasturing us, providing for us food and drink, and defending us with his life. The Father has entrusted us to Jesus for whom we are more precious than all else (see John 10:29). How precious must we be that our true life can be nourished on nothing less than God himself in Jesus! Who could ever have believed that we would be given him as food and drink? "I came that they may have life, and have it abundantly" (John 10:10).

Julian of Norwich expressed her profound insight into God's passionate, tender caring for us in terms of motherhood:

> The mother can give her child to suck of her milk. But our precious Mother Jesus, he can feed us with himself; and does this most courteously and tenderly, with the Blessed Sacrament which is our life. And with all the sweet sacraments he sustains us mercifully and graciously....
>
> The mother can lay her child tenderly to her breast, but our tender Mother Jesus can lead us, homely, into his blessed breast, by his sweet open side; and show us there, in part, the Godhead and the joys of heaven, with a spiritual sureness of endless bliss....
>
> This fair, lovely word "Mother," it is so sweet and so knit to our nature, that it cannot be said to any or of any, but to him who is very Mother of life and of all. The kind, loving mother understands and knows the needs of her child. She looks after it tenderly as is the nature of motherhood....

Oftentimes, when our falling and our wretchedness are shown to us, we are afraid, and so greatly ashamed of ourselves, that we scarcely know where to put ourselves. Yet even then, our courteous Mother does not want us to run away: nothing could displease him more. Rather, he wants us to behave as a child. For when it is distressed and afraid, it runs quickly to its mother. And if it can do nothing else, it cries to the mother for help, with all its might. So will he have us behave as the meek child, saying: "My Mother, my loving Mother, my gracious Mother, my dear Mother, have mercy on me. I have made myself foul and unlike you; and I cannot or may not put it right without your help and grace."...It is his will, then, that we behave as a child, who naturally trusts in the love of its mother, in weal and woe.

(Julian of Norwich)

15

NO GREATER LOVE

There is no doubt whatsoever that Jesus dreaded the suffering he was to undergo. He did not want to die. Those close to him must have witnessed more than once his all-too-human shrinking from what lay before him: "In the days of his flesh, Jesus offered up prayers and supplications, with loud cries and tears, to the one who was able to save him from death" (Heb 5:7). How poignant this glimpse of our beloved Lord terrified of suffering and death! Peter touched a raw nerve when, on Jesus solemnly warning his disciples of the ordeals to come, he officiously took his Master aside to reassure him: he must put these dark thoughts away, such things were not to happen! Jesus reacted as if stung: "Get behind me, Satan!" (Matt

not tell us so, but what follows seems strongly to suggest extreme tension in Jesus.

Uncharacteristically, Jesus does not consent to see these men, does not come face-to-face with them. Why? "The hour has come for the Son of Man to be glorified" (John 12:23), yes, but only by way of suffering and death. Jesus must die, die to all earthly success, to all that human nature esteems, to his earthly existence, if he is to become the world's redeemer. God's human voice, which echoed round the hills and across the Sea of Galilee, must be silenced in death. His yes to death, to utter powerlessness, is that "word of power" that upholds the universe (see Heb 1:3).

Jesus's yes was not without struggle, however: "Now my soul is troubled. And what should I say—'Father, save me from this hour'? No, it is for this reason that I have come to this hour" (John 12:27). "Do you think that I cannot appeal to my Father, and he will at once send me more than twelve legions of angels? But how then would the scriptures be fulfilled, which say it must happen in this way?" (Matt 26:53–54). In some early Renaissance paintings of the passion, above the sordid earthly scene of men scourging Jesus, crowning him with thorns, and making fun of him, angels career wildly, howling with outrage and grief at what is being done to their beloved Lord, the Lord of Glory.

They would swoop down to rescue him but may not do so. Nothing can destroy their Lord's love for these terrible human creatures torturing him and heaping ignominies upon him: "They do not know what they are doing" (Luke 23:34). Having become one of them, he will stand by them to the very end and will share the lot of the "little ones," the powerless, those without privilege and status with no one to defend them. His angels must bow their heads and learn to love those he loves so dearly.

In the midst of his struggle and pain, Jesus turns to us, his chosen friends, urging us to follow him along his way, abandoning our preciously guarded self-possession, throwing ourselves heart and soul into accomplishing the glorious will of the Father, becoming part of the great harvest his dying yields, and in our turn bearing plentiful fruit. "Now is the judgment of this world" (John 12:31). Jesus's obedience unto death is God's way of putting everything right, restoring a lost world, bringing it home to the Father. The rule of the prince of this world is ended.

Christ Crucified

16

LOVE IS PATIENT

"Lord, because you were patient in your lifetime, in this chiefly fulfilling the commandment of your Father..." (Thomas à Kempis)—these words from the medieval classic *The Imitation of Christ*, which in my childhood and youth was a well-used book, have always remained with me. Patience, it seems to me, is perhaps the greatest, deepest expression of love. In the lyrical panegyric of true love's qualities found in 1 Corinthians 13—which we can be sure was the disciples' answer to the question, "What was he like, what was Jesus like?"—patience heads the list: "Love is patient..." (1 Cor 13:4).

Patience is kind, does not insist on its own way; it is not irritable or resentful; patience bears all things, believes all things, hopes all things, endures to the end. Jesus was utterly poor in spirit, the perfect Child of the Father accepting from the Father's hand his humanity in its limited, weak, and vulnerable condition. We have within us ingrained ways of mitigating our poverty and for that reason cannot readily perceive that to be human is to be poor in the deepest sense. It means depending for one's very existence on another in a world that we do not control, exposed to the vicissitudes of nature, to suffering of mind, emotion, and body. No one has accepted this condition with such worshipful love as Jesus did.

We reveal even in early childhood an anger that things are not as *I* want them to be and some of us carry throughout our lifetime a deep-down resentment. Our ego insists on having its own way, manipulating other people and circumstances to smooth its path and satisfy its desires. Unless, with Jesus, we lovingly accept the essential poverty of our humanity, acknowledging that our true security and fullness of being are to be found only in the Father's undergirding arms, we can never really love. We will be irritable, quick to take offense, resentful, and unhappy.

Patience is surrender-in-practice to the limitations, frustrations, disappointments, and sorrows of life. Patience endures them to the end. How frequently the letters to the Christian churches in the Book of Revelation speak of the need for patience, for patient endurance if we are to be true disciples and enter the kingdom. We may assume that in his hidden life Jesus experienced and lovingly endured the frustrations—trials small and great— common to human life. We have firsthand witness of his conduct in his public ministry.

The Twelve were always with him, night and day. They observed his unfailing patience with the crowds who flocked to him, his gentle kindness face-to-face with human frailties. Jesus and his disciples had definitively left house and home and were itinerant, dependent as they went from village to village on friends and well-wishers for food and shelter. Not infrequently they were left without food and with nowhere to lay their heads (see Luke 9:58). There were days when they had no time to eat, so hungry they were glad to eat raw corn (see Mark 2:23).

The disciples' anger burst out when a town refused to receive their Master, and they wanted to call down fire from heaven to consume the inhabitants. It would seem that people thought only of their own needs and were indifferent to Jesus's fatigue; he was taken advantage of, as we say. Jesus did not think so; he remained patiently, lovingly welcoming. For this he had come. Yet how many occasions there were for irritation, for taking offense! It seems he never wearied of quietly disputing with the Pharisees in an effort to convince them of his mission. He longed for their surrender. The sneers, the contempt, the nasty insinuations of his enemies must have wounded him, for in deriding him they were dishonoring, wounding, the Father in whose place he stood. A drunkard and a glutton! (see Luke 7:34). A sorcerer! The very King of Heaven a sorcerer! Accused of casting out devils by Beelzebub, the prince of devils, he does not take offense but responds with an appeal to common sense (see Luke 11:14–23). Fire from heaven to consume these blasphemers? No, our humble Lord quietly asserts that whatever blasphemies are uttered against him, the lowly Son of Man, are forgivable (see Matt 12:32).

Jesus understood the human heart and the deep fears and anxieties that lay behind their enmity and desire to be rid of him.

Christ Crucified

17

TAKE MY LIFE

While this reflection is addressed to religious women, its wisdom is universal. In giving the gift of ourselves in any life commitment, we are making a radical expression of trust that the Lord will bring us to fulfillment within the boundaries of that commitment. Our trust in God is enacted and our fulfillment realized as, inspired by grace, we choose not to cling to the demands of the ego but rather to surrender in love to the needs of others.

When God inspires us to consecrate ourselves to him by the three vows of chastity, poverty, and obedience, he is calling us to enter into the kenosis of his Son in an explicit, radical way. What these vows are saying is, I hand myself over to you, my God. From now on, I give up self-determination, that great gift of freedom to make my own choices, to decide for myself, to shape my own life. This great gift I hand back to you, wanting you to govern my life from morning to night, every day of my life. With Jesus I want your will to be my food and drink, that by which I live.

You have given me the right to possess a measure of earthly goods that would give me some control over my life and enable me to be fulfilled as a woman. To possess even a small portion of material things gives me the possibility of self-expression in the way I dress, the books I read, in my occupation and entertainment. I hand back to you this right you have given me. I know that I can trust you to give me all I need to become the person you created me to be without this normal means.

I yield to you the right you have given me to marry and bear children. To renounce the status, dignity, and joy of wifehood and motherhood is indeed a great sacrifice and one it would be folly, indeed dangerous, to make did you not ask it of me and pledge yourself to bring me to womanly fulfillment in my union with you. You are my beloved and through union with you I will become fruitful, a mother of many children.

Only one who is God could ask the radical renunciation of beautiful, precious things that are the elixir of life, for he alone can and will replenish the stripped and wounded heart with treasures of love beyond our imagining, treasures that will satisfy to the full and forever its deepest needs.

As with Our Lady's *fiat*: "Body and soul I belong to the Lord, let him do what he will with me" (see Luke 1:38), the gift of ourselves, expressed in the vows, is unconditional. We have no idea of what lies ahead, of what will be asked of us. Neither did Our Blessed Lady when she gave her consent, but our trust is, as was hers, not in ourselves but in Our Lord. We trust him utterly, knowing he will give us all we need to meet the hour and its demands. Like her, however, we must constantly ponder on God's word, cultivate an attentiveness, an awareness, so that at every moment we know what we are doing and why we are doing it. It is important for us to watch over our thoughts and movements of desire. When we recognize that our will is straying to selfish regard, we redirect it. There can be no holiday from this loving attention.

Only God can wrest us from our ego-possession. Our first thought, naturally speaking, is always for *me*, how does this affect *me*? Will she be kind to *me*? Our grace-inspired reaction must be: I do not matter; God matters, other people, my sisters, they matter; what does it matter if I am tired, not feeling very well, unhappy? How pleasing to Our Lord is this constant effort to unself ourselves! It is the *practical* way of loving. "Endeavor, my child, always to do the will of another rather than your own will" (Thomas à Kempis). A precious maxim! Community life gives us never-ending opportunities for choosing God rather than self, for this is what we do when we put others first, their wishes, their needs, before our own.

To understand the vows means understanding that we no longer belong to ourselves but to our community and in this way to God. Body, strength, talents, time, energy, are for our community first of all and, under obedience, for others, not for ourselves. I am a servant, with no rights. Servant! Our Savior's chosen word! Can there be a higher state than servanthood since this is what our God chose for himself? Every time we go out of self to others, we allow God to come into us, and he works within us at a level of our being of which normally we are not aware. He wants us to "forget" even our "soul," that is, our truest, deepest self, renouncing curiosity as to our spiritual state. This is the sphere of divine operation that our nosiness can spoil.

Our sole longing and aim must be to fulfill the Father's holy will, allowing him to forge us as he wills and use us as he wills for the world's sanctification.

Christ Crucified

18

SURPASSING ALL UNDERSTANDING

"The glory that you have given me I have given them" (John 17:22). We hear these words, we read these words, here I am writing them down, and they make scarcely any emotional impact on me, no more than when I listen to or read of the mysteries of the universe. Their magnitude numbs my faculties. If we could grasp the meaning of Jesus's words, if we had but a glimpse of the reality they express, I suspect we would die of joy. Our frail nature could not bear the weight of glory of which they speak.

What is the glory that the Father gives to Jesus? Surely everything the Father himself is and has, with nothing held back. It would seem that "glory" is the Holy Spirit, the offspring of the union of love between Father and Son. The evangelist John, in one way or another, leads us to the realization that we, poor earthlings, are immersed in the life of the Holy Trinity. The Father gives Jesus everything; Jesus gives everything to us. Why? O why? The answer can only be because God wants the joy of sharing his blissful, glorious existence with us. God *wants* us, God *yearns* for us, and this yearning for us is the cause of our yearning for him:

You would call, and I would answer you;
You would long for the work of your hands.
(Job 14:15)

Desire for God is indelibly engraved in the basic substance of our being in the form of the universal longing for perfect happiness. Why should we long for happiness, why even recognize it as a longing, unless it is there to be had? We are "for-God," such is our deepest identity and meaning. What else is desire but a reaching out for what we love? To *be* desire, to be a desiring being, is to be made for love; love is our very meaning and the love of God "has been poured into our hearts through the Holy Spirit that has been given to us" (Rom 5:5). We desire God because God desires us and has chosen to need us for his perfect happiness.

Jesus tells us that he is the food we need if we are to live, eat me! He is the living water, without which we die of thirst, drink me! As Good Shepherd, he seeks us in grievous pain. He thirsts for us with a thirst we alone can allay but "you refuse to come to me to have life" (John 5:40). This ardent longing, this passion of love, is expressed outwardly in the torments of his sacred passion, in sweat of blood in the garden, in cry of thirst on the cross.

"All for us," yes, but this means for each one of us in particular, and each one of us may and must affirm: Jesus loves me as he loves no one else, loves me uniquely as his "only one." Everything he has done he has done for me; for me he died and gladly. All he offers he offers to me. My Lover is my God. My God is my Lover, passionately in love with me. I must believe it, though that does not mean that I must feel it. What can life mean for me except to receive his love? To receive him I must be "there" and I am "there" when I do always what pleases him in thought, word, and deed. Jesus in his saving work can be in the world only through individual hearts yielded up to him. Use everything he gives you, the demands of your vocation, all the circumstances of life, and above all the sacraments. Nowhere is the power of Christ, his transforming love, so available to us as in the sacraments.

Crist Crucified

19

THE POWERLESSNESS OF GOD

We often hear it said, "If there were a God these dreadful things would not happen. A good, all-powerful God would *act, do something* to stop the natural calamities that cause untold human suffering, put an end to appalling human cruelties." No doubt our own hearts have raised anxious questions: Why is God so silent in the face of great human suffering? Is God powerless? Faith knows the answer, but it is not an answer that satisfies merely human reason.

Perhaps the first religious act of a Catholic infant is to make the sign of the cross with the words, "In the name of the Father and of the Son and of the Holy Spirit." What a wealth of theology lies in this act! When the all-holy God chose to reveal his inmost self to us in order to draw us to himself, it was in a form that human pride and wisdom despise, namely, that of weakness and humiliation; in a self-emptying love that left him destitute, left him dying on the cross, naked, covered with wounds, humiliated and degraded in the eyes of the world. What can we do but fall down and worship this baffling mystery, this expression of a lavish, extravagant love? Nothing else could adequately reveal to us, self-contained, self-seeking, and self-determining creatures that we are, the *truth*, the *reality*, of God. Left to ourselves we form an image of a god in our own likeness but on a large scale. This god would control the world, coerce with benevolent power, and make life easier for us, whereas the living and true God has revealed himself as absolute Love. Love never coerces.

Through the redeeming incarnation we are given a glimpse of the trinitarian life of God, a life of total self-bestowal that it is our blessed destiny to share. The Father *Is*, exists in begetting the Son, in pouring himself out to him, and the Son *Is* by returning all to the Father. In a way incapable of image or expression, the Spirit *Is* this mutual self-dispossession with which the Father endows his Son and the Son his Father. "All that the Father has is mine" (John 16:15); "all mine are yours, and yours are mine" (John 17:10). "In the image of God he created them; male and female he created them" (Gen 1:27).

We cannot be true to our humanity made in the image of God unless we live a life like God's life of self-expropriation in bestowal to others. We can become our true selves only by giving ourselves away, living for God and for others. To cling to self, to remain in self, can end only in death, in a hell of our own choosing. True life, eternal life, is life in communion, for the fount of all existence is communion: "that they may all be one. As you, Father, are in me and I am in you" (John 17:21). "In the image of God he created them"!

How deeply St. Paul entered into this mystery! To him was revealed the unsearchable riches of Christ and the human vocation to be "in Christ." He saw and lived the practical consequences of this. Jesus had promised his apostles a share in the chalice of his suffering (see Matt 20:23) and in the letters of St. Paul we get a glimpse of the share that was his, see, for example, 2 Corinthians 1:8–11; 11:16–33; and 12:5–10. The encounter with the risen Lord shattered the self-assured, self-righteous Saul; stricken with an incurable wound, like Jacob before him (see Gen 32:24–28), he went his way limping, no longer Saul but Paul. Face-to-face with Jesus, his spiritual destitution was revealed to him. He confronted his sinfulness and total inability to save himself. The image of God he had inherited or fashioned for himself was shattered:

I had heard of you by the hearing of the ear,
    but now my eye sees you;
therefore I despise myself, and repent in dust
    and ashes. (Job 42:5–6)

Rather than sinking into despair he learned to "boast" of his weakness, knowing that Christ's power would be free to work, and that magnificently, through his very weakness. "Whenever I am weak, then I am strong" (2 Cor 12:10). This does not mean he experienced *himself* as strong, most likely he continued to feel weak and fearful, but he was certain that the *divine* weakness and powerlessness of love by which we were redeemed was invincible. The saint of Lisieux had a profound understanding of this paradox. The poorer we are, without inner resources, the more Jesus can work in us. She is emphatic that the greatest of all the graces God gave her was to show her her weakness and to inspire her with an unshakeable trust in his infinite mercy. The more wretched we are, the more God is free to give himself to us, provided we accept our poverty and throw ourselves in total trust into the arms of his merciful love. "O my Divine Sun, I am happy to feel myself so small and frail in your presence and my heart is at peace" (St. Thérèse of Lisieux).

Silent, hidden, powerless Love, the world does not recognize you but by your gift we recognize you and fall in silent worship. We entreat you to draw us, wrest us away from our self-centered selves and assume us into yourself. May we seek ourselves in nothing, but by living by you and in you, devote ourselves entirely to the fulfillment of your holy will. O humble, powerless Love, yours is the kingdom, the power, and the glory forever and ever!

CHRIST CRUCIFIED

20

A SONG OF LOVE

Blessed, blessed be our God,
enduring joy and jubilation,
opening to us the fathomless depths
of your merciful heart!
How can I praise your majesty and beauty,
powerful and glorious?
You fashioned with your holy hands
the whole created world,
and every creature you have made
cries aloud how beautiful you are
Mysterious Holy Trinity!

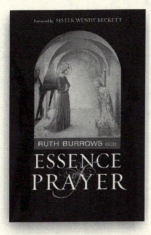

ESSENCE OF PRAYER

Ruth Burrows, OCD, with a foreword by Sr. Wendy Beckett

Prayer is a word we take for granted. Ought we to do so? What do we mean by prayer? What does the word mean in the Christian context? Almost always when we talk about prayer we refer to something we do. From that standpoint, questions problems, confusion, discouragement and illusions multiply. For Ruth Burrows it is essential to correct this view.

In this simple but profoundly insightful book we find the richness of vision of a contemplative nun whose message counteracts the tendency of so much modern writing about the spiritual life.

224 pages • 5 ⁷/₁₆ x 8 ½ • 1-58768-039-4
Paperback • $17.95

GUIDE-LINES FOR MYSTICAL PRAYER

Ruth Burrows, OCD

When first published in 1976, and still relevant today, this critically acclaimed work of spiritual theology as reflection on spiritual experience was a growing trend; but at the same time there was a new interest in, and a return to, the classical Carmelite theology of prayer, with an effort to formulate that theology in contemporary thought categories. *Guidelines for Mystical Prayer* embodies both tendencies. It offers a personal narrative, a reflection on the spiritual history of two gifted people, St. Teresa and St. John of the Cross; and yet it speaks clearly out of the Carmelite tradition, and in the language of today.

160 pages • 5 1/8 x 7 3/4 • 978-0-8091-5358-9
Paperback • $16.95

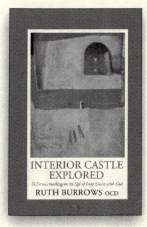

INTERIOR CASTLE EXPLORED

St. Teresa's Teaching on the Life of Deep Union with God

Ruth Burrows, OCD

A penetrating interpretation of St. Teresa of Avila's central teaching on prayer. But it is more than a contemporary Carmelite commentary on the 16th-century Carmelite classic; it is also, in its own right, a guide to the life of deep union with God.

128 pages • 5 ⅛ x 7 ¾ • 978-1-58768-046-5
Paperback • $14.00

TO BELIEVE IN JESUS

Ruth Burrows, OCD

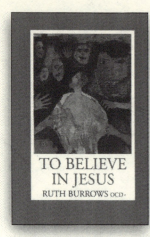

This best selling author writes particularly for lay people about contemplation and the life of prayer. The message of *To Believe in Jesus* is heartening, if disconcerting, for it stands a common assumption on its head. The way to holiness is not through dramatic renunciation, and holiness itself is not just for the "specialists," clergy, and religious. Holiness cannot be struggled for and won - it can only be given, and all that is necessary is that we should ask. As soon as we cease to strive for virtue, concentrating attention uselessly on ourselves, and instead recognize our weakness, our need, the way is open to encounter God and the holiness of Jesus which is His gift.

128 pages • 5 x 7 ¾ • 978-1-58768-065-6
Paperback • $16.00